A BOUND
WOMAN
IS A
DANGEROUS
THING

BY THE SAME AUTHOR

The Fluid Boundaries of Suffrage and Jim Crow:
Staking Claims in the American Heartland

\Vi-zə-bəl\\Teks-chərs

A BOUND WOMAN IS A DANGEROUS THING

The Incarceration of
African American Women from
Harriet Tubman to Sandra Bland

DaMaris B. Hill

BLOOMSBURY PUBLISHING
NEW YORK • LONDON • OXFORD • NEW DELHI • SYDNEY

BLOOMSBURY PUBLISHING
Bloomsbury Publishing Inc.
1385 Broadway, New York, NY 10018, USA

BLOOMSBURY, BLOOMSBURY PUBLISHING, and the Diana logo are trademarks of
Bloomsbury Publishing Plc

First published in the United States 2019

Copyright © DaMaris B. Hill, 2019

ISBN: HB: 978-1-63557-261-2; eBook: 978-1-63557-262-9

Library of Congress Cataloging-in-Publication Data is available

4 6 8 10 9 7 5 3

Designed by Tree Abraham
Printed and bound in the U.S.A. by Berryville Graphics Inc., Berryville, Virginia

To find out more about our authors and books visit www.bloomsbury.com
and sign up for our newsletters.

Bloomsbury books may be purchased for business or promotional use.
For information on bulk purchases please contact Macmillan Corporate and
Premium Sales Department at specialmarkets@macmillan.com.

To my ancestors, blood relatives or otherwise

CONTENTS

Preface

"Between 1980 and 2016 the number of incarcerated women increased by more than 700%." —The Sentencing Project

Reading about the Black women in *A Bound Woman Is a Dangerous Thing* will not comfort. These poems honor Black women who have had experiences with incarceration. They were inspired by current events and historical framings of Black women freedom fighters—such as Harriet Tubman, Assata Shakur, and Sandra Bland—some of whom have organized or inspired resistance movements over the last two centuries. Many of the poems detail the violent consequences Black women endure while engaged in individual and collective acts of resistance.

My grandmother's picture opens this book. As far as I know, she was never formally incarcerated. I chose to honor her because the Jane Crow styles of oppression prevalent during her lifetime were careful to include violence or threats of violence for accessing civil liberties. These oppressions were rooted in false ideas of social superiority that could make one "feel" imprisoned. Jane Crow types of oppression could also affect one's mental health, inciting mania or mental illness. Fracture a wise woman's intellect. As they did to so many other Black women in America, the violently enforced codes of Jane Crow oppression placed restrictions on my grandmother's body, and inadvertently on her mind.

In a world seemingly so absent of love and justice, some have chosen to defensively armor themselves with ambivalence. Who can blame them? We all feel the ricochets of injustice savaging the landscape. The pain and urgency of our collective hurt make it easy for some to believe that our present-day human rights movements, like Black Lives Matter, are a result of recent police shootings and civil brutalities. I caution against this; the Black Lives Matter movement and the Blue Lives Matter movement and the All Lives Matter movement are shrapnel in the long and rarely acknowledged American presumption that Black people are less than human. As a result of this presumption, Black women have been heavily invested in abolition, protest, and resistance movements aimed at the acknowledgment of Black humanity. Some of these movements began in the colonial era. Writing poems about such women has forced me to question what it means for a Black woman to engage in resistance within this particular time and this specific space. I concluded that it means that I must give myself permission to love, wail, weep, grieve, call on ancestors, begin a daily ritual of resistance—even if it is rooted in my fears. It means understanding the fluidity of my emotions—like wanting to grab a gun and turn it toward my threats, before setting it inside my mouth, and then finally locking it away. The undervaluing of Black humanity is witnessed by millions when Ms. Diamond Reynolds and her daughter, loved ones of Philando Castile, grab a cellphone camera and collect evidence of Philando's death—an act of love. Sharing grief. Bearing witness. For several months, I have been asking myself, "What will my tears record today?"

I stand here, bound in a legacy of love, in the midst of the ricochet, in solidarity with the hurt and wounded, whether they occupy this life or the next—like: Gynnya McMillen / Sandra Bland / Freddie Gray / Samuel DuBose / Sharonda Coleman-Singleton / Cynthia Hurd / DePayne Middleton-Doctor / Miz Susie Jackson and her cousin Miz Ethel Lance / Senator Reverend Clementa Pinckney / Tywanza Sanders / Reverend Doctor Daniel Simmons Sr. / Pastor Myra Thompson / Eric Garner / Trayvon Martin / Tamir Rice / Eric Harris / Walter Scott / Jonathan Ferrell / Renisha McBride / Philando Castile and . . .

The afflicted pray for healing—just as hungry people pray for bread, but when has God ever sent bread? In my recollection of the scriptures, God has always sent a woman. A woman like Eve and the unnamed woman that preceded her. A woman like Moses's mother, Jochebed, and the woman who raised him to be a king, Bithia. A woman like Deborah and her skull-piercing homegirl, Jael. Maybe some manna, but when has God ever sent bread?

The poet Lucille Clifton advises me to "study the masters." In this way, my work reflects a historical lineage of resistance and my deep study of writers such as Phillis Wheatley, Anna Julia Cooper, Frances Ellen Watkins Harper, Gwendolyn Brooks, Toni Morrison, Lucille Clifton. In kind, my work does not ignore the literary inheritances of other writers, like Henry David Thoreau, Walt Whitman, Ernest Hemingway, and James Baldwin. Using history as inspiration, my work is immersed in a profoundly American literary tradition. This tradition explores the realities of the American condition and is in dialogue with ideas of democracy.

These poems are love letters. The opening of the book explores how I am bound in the sense of being beholden to others. In the African American tradition, we honor our ancestors. My grandmother was inspirational to me. In her home were two leather-bound Bibles, the most gorgeous books that I have ever seen. My favorite had a brown exterior that was ornately designed using pyrography. The book itself was like so many of us, beautifully scarred. Scriptures were printed in the center of the pages and the borders contained colored illustrations of the biblical stories and angels. The front pages of the Bible do not begin with the shaping of the heavens and the earth; they start with the ancestors. In this Bible our family records our full names, professions, places of residence, births, marriages, and transitions of our family members. The nearly two thousand pages of this Bible glitter. My grandmother was the "keeper" of this Bible, taking on the role of both librarian and archivist. She could not keep my cousins and me away from it. We wanted to interact with it constantly. My fingers stained with peanut butter and jelly pressed into the pages. Realizing that the "family" Bible brought us so much pleasure, my grandma purchased a children's Bible. It was bound in white leather and illustrated. It had several hundred pages. We found it to be a disappointment compared to the family Bible.

These first books, these Bibles, continue to influence my writing. I've included images in this book and the poems reference many biblical stories. They contain "echo" poems that are distinct lyrical conversations with Lucille Clifton's poetry that are particularly inspiring. As a graduate student, I studied the ways Clifton illustrated women in her works, particularly in spiritual contexts. I follow my poems honoring Clifton's literary legacy by writing a tribute poem to her great-grandmother. I used Clifton's rendering of her great-grandmother "Lucy" in *Generations* as inspiration. Within this context of being beholden, I wanted to open this book by reflecting on legacies, the things we bring with us to the writing. In doing so, I honor two people that influenced my literary career.

The second section of this book looks to the idea of being fettered, restrained with irons or imprisoned. I am so genuinely moved by the triumphs and tragedies these Black women endured within the justice system. While researching the historical intersections between Black women and incarceration, I was introduced to *Colored Amazons: Crime, Violence, and Black Women in the City of Brotherly Love, 1880–1910*, written by Kali Nicole Gross, PhD, a professor of history at Rutgers University. I immediately began drafting poems about the women featured in Gross's book. Black women who earned substantially less money than their peers. Black women who aimed to liberate themselves from discrimination and were imprisoned while journeying toward freedom. I found Gross's work to be a substantial and necessary history. Therefore the book became a source of ekphrastic inspiration.

Most of the poems attempt to create first-person testimonies and are in formal verse. The use of formal poetic structure is symbolic of the women's physical confinement. The formal poem structures also act as a critique of the economic and democratic limitations many African American women experienced in Philadelphia. Philadelphia is depicted as the beacon of liberty for Americans, but ironically it became the exact opposite for many of the African American women who migrated there.

The third portion of the book reflects on the ways some women are bound to words and use their writings as weapons. These women are bound to the ways they write, mark, or set boundaries to draw a line in the sand. In all these ways, they set themselves apart. Many of the women in this section are writers and/or political activists who used their tools to protest. In Ida B. Wells's poem, a lyrical narrative emerges within mathematically rationalized form. The poem presents itself this way in order to honor her professional career as a journalist and statistical social scientist. Wells used her talents to actively protest lynching. She is followed by Zora Neale Hurston because Hurston used her education as a writer and anthropologist to challenge the ways African Americans were being dehumanized scientifically. Claudia Jones followed in the legacy of Wells by using journalism and economic histories to document the injustices against African Americans, particularly Black women. Her work focused on how the United States uses race as a way to disenfranchise Black women citizens. Eartha Kitt used her celebrity and political access to protest the Vietnam War, which she felt killed far too many young Black boys. This chapter also includes a poem about Sonia Sanchez's continued work as an activist. Sanchez banded together with grandmothers around the country to demand that military recruiting offices accept their own enlistment rather than enlist the protestors' grandchildren into war. This section ends with Sandra Bland. Months before her traffic stop and murder, she began a social media series entitled #SandySpeaks to protest police brutality and aid in Black Lives Matter efforts.

Section four focuses on what it means to hurdle; to spring forth. In this section I question when and in what ways it is necessary to protest and exercise action in a defensive posture. How many times did Harriet Tubman spring forth and leave plantations with the intention of breaking the law as a means of emancipating people? How many times did she evade the patrollers as a means of survival? She did this so often that the authorities posted a reward for her arrest. Also springing forth are Joan Little and Ruby McCollum, women who liberated themselves from their respective rapists. Fannie Lou Hamer hurdles forth from the oppression associated with being a sharecropper experiencing Jane Crow political and social oppression. She became a community activist who participated in the Democratic National Convention, voter rights campaigns, and the freedom movement. Finally, the chapter looks to Grace Jones and the ways she abstracted and performed race, gender, and sexuality in pop culture, complicating and expanding the notions of Black womanhood.

The fifth section embraces the connotations associated with hemming in—being tucked into the fabric. This section is about the life and legacy of Assata Shakur. A woman like Assata Shakur could have been nurtured only under the social and cultural constraints of America. To me she is a second Harriet Tubman, a hyperintelligent, spiritually strong, visionary, loving Black woman who was and is also committed to freeing people who are in social or political bondage. She is not a murderer. There is no evidence that she murdered or shot anyone, particularly the state police officers who pulled over the car she was in. Before Shakur could exit the car as the state police requested, she was shot through her shoulder with a double-barrel shotgun. According to medical examiners and the court, Shakur was shot when her hands were raised in the air, as the officers requested. Considering the evidence, I am puzzled why the mention of her name continues to paralyze people with fear. She is no bogeyman. What is it about a Black woman bound to her own liberation that makes people terrified of their own shadows, their own darkness? In the pre-emancipated South of 1856, there was a $40,000 reward offered for Harriet Tubman's capture. "Dead or alive," the ads stated. In 2017, that $40,000 in U.S. currency would be worth $1,101,670.36. The reward for capturing the FBI's Most Wanted, Assata Shakur, recently increased from 1,000,000 to 2,000,000 U.S. dollars. Assata Shakur's net worth probably does not total $2,000,000. She may never earn that amount of money over her lifetime. Again, I am perplexed. What is so threatening about a Black woman bound to her own freedom, one who is also committed to the liberation of others?

The final chapter explores ideas associated with connections. This section talks about a specific type of bond, the bond between generations, parenthood. Although I did not know Gynnya McMillen, I look upon her as a daughter of this era, a kind of extended family member. For me she is an example of the perverse criminalization of Black girls. She was imprisoned in Kentucky, in a state with the second-highest incarceration rate for women in the nation (Nicole D. Porter, The Sentencing Project). How many girls are sent to prison in this rush for free labor? She died in a state that politicians view as a model for national incarceration efforts. Gynnya is remembered, is honored, because she is a daughter. She is a girl who was arrested for having an altercation with her mother. Seventeen hours after her arrest she was found dead in her jail cell. In this life and the next, Gynnya is loved. As a mother, sister, aunt, cousin, teacher, member of an extended community, I wish we cared for her better.

The other poems in this section are poems for my son, who is living and suffering. The section begins with "Patriot and Prisoner." This monologue marks the point in the book where I stop referencing history and I begin an autobiographical journey about how the recent murders of Black men and protest movements psychologically unfolded in my mind. "Patriot and Prisoner" demonstrates the tensions I feel between my allegiance to my identity as a United States service member and my commitment as a mother of a Black child. It discusses my experiences serving in the United States Air Force and contrasts them with my experiences as a mother of a civilian who happens to be a Black man and a target of police brutality and the racist backlash that is articulated as political and social psychological violence. These poems are personal to me. My son was a promising student, popular in his community, and he demonstrated exceptional political promise. He was postracial. During the recent forty-fifth presidential race and subsequent election, the stress of police threats, the racist cultural climate, and the all-out defacement of democracy, he began coping, like many people, by using substances, resulting in addiction. The poems question what are the ripple effects and losses of the immediate inequalities and killings associated with the Black Lives Matter era.

Like history, I am older than I look. My white ancestors immigrated to this country in the 1780s; my African ancestors were here before them. My mother was in labor with me in 1974. She and my father wished for a son they thought would unite them. I came, a woman in the body of a girl, three-and-a-half weeks late, breaking my mother in too many ways. She hadn't the energy to name me. My father was too lazy to be original; he scribbled my mother's name on the certificate and wrote the name of his mother right behind the wife's name. This ritual of naming is one way we learn to love and bind with people who no longer share the planet with us.

In these poems, the legacy of these women's lives chases me like a strong wind. This book is a love letter to women who have been denied their humanity. Most of these women have been forgotten, shunned, and/or erased. Every time I call a name in this book, presume that the person who bears the name is loved. If you are brave, imagine the name of that woman congealing on my tongue, give the names breath and the memory.

Let these women dance among your days and with your nights. Dream better lives.

BOUND

*Harriet Beecher Spruill-Hill, United States
European Command, Patch Barracks in Cold War
Germany (circa 1953)*

Harriet Beecher Spruill-Hill

April 16, 1928 and I don't care to remember

. . . See, I had a grandma who could read at lightning speeds. Now some holy ghost, the best life had for her was this country's second-hand soldier, a loving husband. No room for books and babies at her breasts. The sanctified think marriage is a type of reward if you are a second generation out of slavery color of coffee bean type of woman and your hair is some black lacquer of unruly licorice that has branches that wave like echoes. Her smile whiter than seashells, her breath the scent of tobacco. As narrow as a Carolina pine with worries "'bout the rage of white folks," she died gifting me her photos. The only stories she would write. At birth her name becomes my velvet lush heirloom, tufted behind my mother's.

SHUT UP IN MY BONES
(FOR HARRIET BEECHER SPRUILL-HILL)

I have the racket of anxiety in my genes
It rivets in ink. 'Spite this
I leave these marks. This
evidence of us, undone. In wits'
end, it all ferments and we shape totems
of shame from our amusements.
The musk of my imagination
is as redolent as any untamed woman
and likewise, mistaken for mental illness.

Perfection is a mask, a perfume
in my pulse. I learn to hide
what is feared. To be literate
is to pen oneself with needles, shape beauty
from a funhouse mirror. This is how
artists learn the craft of display.
Call this confession a lie? Look closer.
I stubbed my toe tightrope walking
the lashes of circus clowns.

Only the liberated can see the legacies
of bondage stirring beyond the ribbons.
I have come to know. I am
the savory morsel in America's
teeth. These words are clawed into
the enamel. My face is familiar
among the haints; I wear her likeness
like a caul.

A Bound Woman 4

See, I had a grandma who could read at lightning speeds. Now
some holy ghost, the best life had for her was this country's
secondhand soldier, a loving husband. No room for books and
babies at her breasts. The sanctified think marriage is a type
of reward if you are a second generation out of slavery color of
coffee bean type of woman and your hair is some black lacquer
of unruly licorice that has branches that wave like echoes. Her
smile whiter than seashells, her breath the scent of tobacco.
As narrow as a Carolina pine with worries "'bout the rage of
white folks," she died gifting me her photos. The only stories
she would write. At birth her name becomes my velvet lush
heirloom, tufted behind my mother's.

It is costly to stay free and appear
sane. I am she and an extravagant
kind, a shimmy spilling from
her buttons, the erotic unbridled,
a glimmer riding the golden. I am her
shrill of laughter clapping in doubt.
Curiosity is a coy friend. Chaos,
my alter ego. I mistook a jagged molar
for an ivory tower and I "ain't got
the good sense God gave me
to rot."

*Lucille Clifton and DaMaris Hill at the University of Maryland
in College Park, Maryland (2004)*

Lucille Clifton

[June 27, 1936–February 13, 2010]

Lucille means *light*. Lucille Clifton was born in Depew, New York. She attended Howard University. Robert Hayden, James Baldwin, and Sterling Brown were some of her professors. Chloe Wofford (Toni Morrison) and LeRoi Jones (Amiri Baraka) were her classmates. She married before she graduated and lived in Baltimore, Maryland, for several years. She became the writer in residence at Coppin State College in 1971. Rita Dove refers to Clifton's work as "intellectualized lyricism." I agree. She continues to be funny, generous, and brilliant.

IN THE GARDEN

(an echo poem for Ms. Clifton)

in this garden of marble and men
i swivel slowly in.
i am some clay-faced Janus
following the drums of your tongue.
did you know

these halls are prone to echo?
god is dead, yet the walls
are greedy for confessions.
your words mirror my truth.
forgive me
my voice is a tapestry of tacks
trying to wear the skin of your hymns.

STUDY THE MASTERS
(an echo poem for Ms. Clifton)

i do as you say,
study the masters.
i glean close.
your handiwork of words,
the discipline you command.
All that is huge and hinged with hope
are pressed into me.
i glean closer
chant you in form and line,
recall America,
taste the iron musks of her words.
the clamber of rickety german
and loose latin
always seem to crowd the ear,
collect moist in the eye.

MIZ LUCILLE

(an echo poem for Ms. Clifton)

when I watch you
wrapped up like a bound book
of love letters . . .
surrounded by the smell
of cherished wisdom
or
when I watch you
in two dimensions
backlit and glowing
in a screen much too small to hold you
your light

i say
you, a woman the color of wet sienna,
who wore the truth
as radiant as you?
serving your pain
fragrant as Brook's furious flowers
because of you
i stand up
in the world that gift wrapped me for ruin
i stand up
and mark the script

Portrait of a Young African American Woman

Lucy Sayles

Lucy Sayles was Lucille Clifton's great-grandmother. She is the daughter of Mammy Ca'line, a Dahomey woman. She was mother of Eugene Sayles, whom she conceived with Harvey Nichols. She was the first Black woman granted a trial and subsequently hanged in Virginia. She shot Harvey Nichols off his horse, because their son was born with a withered arm. After shooting him, she waited for the horse to return with the mob to arrest her. Her mother, Mammy Ca'line, had influence in the community and insisted that she be tried as a citizen, rather than lynched by the mob.

LICORICE FOR LUCY
(FOR LUCILLE CLIFTON'S
GREAT-GRANDMOTHER,
LUCILLE SAYLES)

Harvey Nichols always keeps
a pocket full of licorice.
Some gum and glove for Lucy's tongue;
he wants her to hold her mule
outside the doorstep long enough
to jump back and forth across
a broom, time enough for Lucy
to wear his wishes like a veil.

When the South is null
and Confederate nickels are weaker than foil,
some think Nichols is the devil, the same
brand fiend as his friend Abe Lincoln, because
he's a braggart—he has "his Lucy" and he boasts
that she is the one thing in all the South that remains
unbroken. Lucy warns him that a new south
don't make her any more fit
for new masters.

Their son's withered arm is
no omen. It is twin to the tree root
outside of Nichols's house. His white wife
considers the twinning a blessing and stops wishing
for the baby to be baptized in the bleach
water of her wash bin.

Nichols's horse is the only witness.
The beast left the body burning, beside
the sulfur steam of bullet casings and returned
with a mob hungry to remember
the smell of spiced candy. They want to watch
the spittle from Lucy hang like
some soft mirror of a noose.

BOUND.FETTERED.

Three bridesmaids at a wedding in Harlem, 1962

Annie Cutler

On April 22, 1885, Cutler shot and killed her ex-lover, William H. Knight. Cutler's case offers unprecedented insight into working-class black women's values and their feelings of turmoil and powerlessness.

—Kali N. Gross, *Colored Amazons*

THE CONCESSION OF ANNIE CUTLER

Dear Mama, I must go with Knight. I am hell-bound.
Bury me in a white box and my wedding gown.

A remnant of disaster, this grief corsets
my sorrows. Pinch and ball snag in this bride's gown.

The tongue I praised God with was laid upon
Henry. Blasphemy. Betrayal. My gown?

Mama, I swallowed the bitter syrup of angels
unborn as he lingered round my night gown.

I sipped a tea of pennyroyal, primrose
and blue/black cohosh* donning this gown.

Mother. I tasted the bitterness of
three souls, enlivened sacrifices. My gown

defiled, doused in blood stains. Shame suffocates
me like the bodice of my gown.

Mama, bury me in a white box coffin. Cover it
in earth. Darkness has bequeathed this bride's gown,

pulled to hell in passion's chariots. I will be radiant
veiled in vengeance and the singed scorn of a bridal gown,

once white laced adorned with pearls of piety.
The rage smoldering beneath my gratuitous gown

of rejection and the fallacy of Henry's promises.
I am forsaken as his bride processes in her white gown.

Her lips plump with smiles and secrets that once belonged to me.
She a fine portrait of domesticity framed and fringed in her gown

round with his child, the glee of Henry. Fury engulfs me,
a picture of ruined antiquity, an abandoned Venus in a torn gown.

Mama, I choose Hell to be my grand ball of debauchery
and will stand honorably as the flames feast on my bride's gown.

I, Annie Cutler, Juliet of Henry Knight, will kill him and myself
in spite. Please bury me in a white box and my bride's gown.

---

* herbal abortion recipe

A maid at work

Alice Clifton

Given the circumstances, Clifton's case not only offers insight into the impact of slavery on black womanhood but also showcases the impossible position of women like her. Clifton sought to escape slavery by slashing her infant's throat . . .

—Kali N. Gross, *Colored Amazons*

THE LOVE SONG OF ALICE CLIFTON

vexed with wickedness, lies as promises,
Philadelphia-visceral. without joy,
a raven's caw warning black mistresses.
Schaffer's pale, he a lowly cherub, coy.
pleas for liberty twisted in his tongue,
promised to unbind me. loose, as his wife.
my ears cradle fetal desires. freedom
Schaffer whispers "take that honeyed babe's life."
amity pokes me twice. his a sweet prod.
still born was our lust. still. i did our part.
promised him no bastard chattel of God.
still honey does not cry, nor beats baby's heart.

slashes for dead honey. i'm bound and blamed.
Schaffer is no savior. our sin, my chains.

Four African American women seated on steps of building at Atlanta University, Georgia (1899 or 1900)

Black Bess

Whereas white men used negative sexual myths to victimize black women with impunity, conversely, black badgers used the "pretense of sex" to victimize white men. By effectively "tricking the tricks," black badgers turned the older script on its head.

—Kali N. Gross, *Colored Amazons*

A MERMAID'S STROLL

Black Bess had a mermaid stroll,
blues and swing with limbs that shimmered.
Ask for a dip and she'd take your toll.
Black Bess had a mermaid stroll,
baited her jelly on your fish pole,
surfed your billfold for her treasure.
Black Bess had a mermaid stroll,
rough up and rob you, while fantasies linger

African American woman (1890s)

Ella Jackson

According to witness testimony, Jackson had been in the house drinking and quarrelling with Johnson throughout the night, and the argument eventually became physical. During the row, Johnson struck Jackson with a lighted lamp that resulted in his death.

—Kali N. Gross, *Colored Amazons*

BEWITCHED

Punching and passion, his love voodoo.
Under his root, I am bound and continue
to pray his kisses don't taste of whiskey.
Pray that if drunk, he would forget me
or take mercy, on yesterday's bruises.

A pint is prisoned, standing in his shoe.
Barefoot and dancing, he sways in blues.
His paws strangle shadows, leaves them achy.
This man's eyes call. His love some type voodoo.

My teeth spill onto the floor. Blood spews.
I kneel before him and beg "just two."
In a trance, we dance, a lamp, Jimmy and
me. Kanzo's flames bring purity,
torching my sorrows. This-a lover's dues.
Jimmy Jackson's love some type voodoo.

---

* In Haitian Voodoo the first level of initiation is the grueling ritual
called *kanzo*, which serves as a rite of passage and symbolizes death
and rebirth into the religion. They [initiates] undergo trial by fire.

Two African American girls sitting on a porch (1900)

Em Lee and Stella Weldon

In 1905, Lee horrified onlookers as she shot and killed her childhood friend Stella Weldon. Born and raised in Scranton, Pennsylvania, both women had attended school and church together and maintained a close relationship until Weldon's marriage.

—Kali N. Gross, *Colored Amazons*

EM LEE'S SWEET ON STELLA

Stella wed Charles and they were Weldon.
She kept from her lovin' and Em Lee.
Secrets and visits, like kisses, seldom.

Those girls stuck on each other like candy,
Sticky sweet!, testifies Bert, Em's brother.
In school, in church. He nods convincingly.

Em's sweet Stella, would there be another?
Sweet Stella—her new baby knows Em's strife.
Sweet Stella—shot dead. No wife. No mother.

One long year Stella lived as Weldon's bride.
Em Lee gunned Stella, speared her baby.
Innocence is evident in Love's cries.

Jealousy and hate embraced Em Lee
as Stella abandoned Lee's seductions.
Love's triangle proves to be mockery.

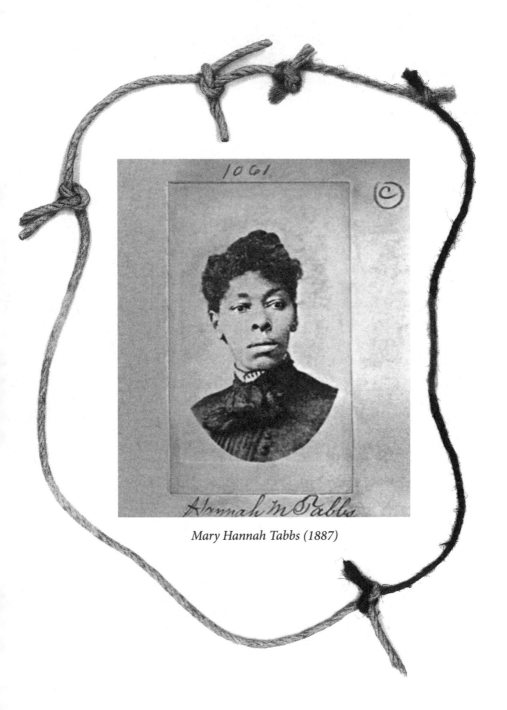

Mary Hannah Tabbs (1887)

Mary Hannah Tabbs

Convicted in the murder of Wakefield Gaines, also black, Mary Hannah Tabbs's crime, extraordinarily brutal, unveiled the extremities of rage, but her well-timed confession and courtroom maneuvering also bear witness to her incisive grasp of the interplay of race, gender, sexuality, and justice.

—Kali N. Gross, *Colored Amazons*

LUSTS AND GAINES

Her right hand raised toward Heaven, he asks if she is Mary Hannah Tabbs
and makes her promise to tell the whole truth as a court's witness.
Her eyes plead mercy from her lap "I can tell you I loved Yella Gaines.
Our love bright as a star, guiding our lives. I his wife. He husband.
Tell you, I fell victim to lust, Yella Gaines and his fancies for Annie.
I can tell you about the fall of a woman, a rainstorm of regret, a phony letter

written by a ghost and my weary heart." She sighs, "The letter."
She rocks between her memories. The jury sifts. Mrs. Tabbs
speaks. "The letter was written by Yella Gaines. He signed Annie's
name. Left me a grieving woman. We betrayed by Wilson. He's no witness."
Wilson calls Mary a hell-bound harlot, screaming that John Tabbs is her
    husband.
"John abandoned me. My righteousness and reason gulfed in one kiss from
    Gaines.

God's wrath rests in the lusts of this wretch. I will forever thirst for Yella Gaines,
a passion that scorches my heart and tortures my soul. His forged letter
belched that he loved Annie more than he desired to be my husband.
He would prey on her. Sweet Jesus. Abandoned again. Just like John Tabbs.
His fingers wicked vines of deception. Dowson's Cynara,* a witness,
a tale of love and morals. I was betrayed by Yella Gaines and my niece, Annie.

My sorrow is a migrant southerner. It trailed me to Philadelphia. Me, nor Annie
escaped. My niece was raised in my sorrow's and shadows, in the glow of
    Gaines.
I am guilty of lucid heart, one whose fury spills from this witness

---

* "Cynara," Ernest Dowson (1867–1900)

stand in tears. Why did Yella Gaines have to write that letter?
As a reminder that he could never love me, an old maid, Mary Tabbs?
That master's mulatto bastard was no man, and no better than my black-hearted
    husband.

Gaines' words like cinnamon candy. He said, *I walk too wide to have an old*
    husband.
My hips *round enough to make a meek man out of Lucifer.* Annie
was still a girl when Yella Gaines whispered that I forget John Tabbs.
Then he lie between my niece and I, our bloodline his canal. Damn Yella Gaines
and his love for Annie. He could write, signed her name to that letter.
He was going to leave me less than a woman. God, not Wilson, is my witness."

Wilson cries out and declares Mary crazy. He, the prosecution's only witness.
Mary sobs, "John Tabbs was a wicked man and my dreaded husband.
He left me a desperate woman. He ran off. Left no word or letter.
Left me sullen and down. Slumbering in shame and stuck with Annie.
I was a respectable woman tempted by the firefly ambers of Yella Gaines's
golden kiss." Is she the ill will of Wakefield Gaines? The judge stares into Tabbs.

"He made me a mockery. I'm his victim. He took my civility." says Mary Hannah
    Tabbs.
"I am guilty of the furies of a fallen woman slain by Satan and golden Gaines.
Wilson killed him. I thanked God for freeing me from passions lashings and
    Annie."

Unidentified young woman wearing gloves,
leaning on prop fence.

Ida Howard

Because black women had few avenues for validation, the smallest sign of disrespect could topple a black woman's carefully constructed, though ultimately fragile, notion of womanhood . . . [Ida] Howard, a twice-convicted badger . . . stabbed a black man to death in broad daylight . . . Howard's vulnerability could not tolerate even this relatively harmless slight [name calling], which apparently, from her vantage, amounted to a grievous offense.

—Kali N. Gross, *Colored Amazons*

WHAT YOU OUGHTA KNOW ABOUT IDA

Ida don't tolerate no disrespect.
One wrong word she'd slice your neck.
Been to Eastern twice as a badger.
She used to punch quick, learned to cut faster.
Her reason and razor all connect.

Stay clear of Ida and that badger sect.
Talk slick to one, you should expect
some form of dreaded disaster.
Ida don't tolerate no disrespect.

Insults do not dissuade or protect.
One wrong stare can send her deject.
Her bitterness and blade are her master.
I testify, she sliced her pastor.
He presumed Ida be less than perfect.
Ida don't tolerate no disrespect.

Eastern State Penitentiary

Laura Williams

Dilapidated conditions magnified sickness, and typhoid, dropsy, and tuberculosis ravaged the institution and resulted in a number of inmates' deaths . . . Laura Williams, a black woman in her early twenties convicted in 1887, died of tuberculosis one month before her sentence ended.

—Kali N. Gross, *Colored Amazons*

STEWING

I dream of hounds. Their teeth loose in my veins.
Their howls consume me. They growl and feast.
She whispers not to run. I can't refrain.

Nightmares of this cell stirring in my brain.
To survive I would suckle possums' teats.
I dream of hounds. Their teeth loose in my veins.

Sweat pours from my body, a heavy rain.
My intestine rotting, rising, my tongue reeks.
She whispers not to run. I can't refrain.

Tuberculosis fevers stew my pain.
Curdle my stomach's bile. Vomit creeps.
I dream of hounds. Their teeth loose in my veins

Awake to my own barking. My voice strained.
The nurse's compress grips me like a leash.
She whispers not to run. I can't refrain.

She tells me to hush as I try to explain.
Stale air of this jail tangled in, death's crease.
I dream of hounds. Their teeth loose in my veins.
She whispers do not run. I can't refrain.

Woman in hat decorated with flowers and striped blouse

Annie Wilson

All but mastering the art of deception, she operated under the alias of Annie Wilson in 1881, when she served her first larceny sentence at Eastern . . . If the true nature of her criminal record would have surfaced, Powell might have entered Eastern as a "thief" and received a sentence longer than a year.

—Kali N. Gross, *Colored Amazons*

FRISK

palms round your jewels
palms your personals, pushing them in her pockets.
palms paper bills and pennies, plopping them in her purse.
palms wave away, past convictions' glare.
palms push two vice cops. they frisk this thrice-time thief.

palms and judge's ears collect "Annie Wilson," an
alias birthed in her throat. palms scribble this name.
a woman is made, a fraud, a first-time offender.

palms brace for the pit. her body shoved into its bowels.
palms pitter patter this place, recalling the cells.
palms pinch 189 days of stench, rotting flesh. she can't stay.
palms fold in prayer, coddling a Sampson-like miracle. she can't stay.
palms push against bars. bones and bruises proof her. she can't stray.

palms, prepare a safe space, in case.
palms are sure to push agony on her sides.
palms, please, place Precious beyond this woman's sins.
palms, protect Precious from the guards.
palms pass her infant between steel, past her stay.

palms and ink, they cling to some things. they
wrestle and prick a baby's breast. they
press. together they tattoo an innocent
into a criminal. a baby, noted with a number, no name.
the cells of her mother pressed upon her.

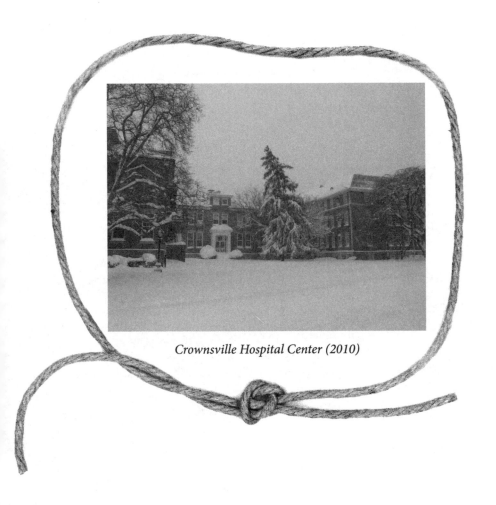

Crownsville Hospital Center (2010)

Black White Criminality in Insane Asylum

Prison records describe a violent, disorderly black female prisoner. Asylum records portray a troubled white female patient . . . Criminality lay largely in the eye of the beholder and those individuals most likely to be gazing did so through a distorted lens.

—Kali N. Gross, *Colored Amazons*

BLACK BIRD MEDLEY

1.
blue veins vine my wrists. rosaries stitch my palms
I pass through Eastern a yellow canary.
my voice, an ebony tongue. hail mary,
no grace. Black soul in the middle like psalms,
my mother's bible songs, a broken heart's balm.
my lips carry her cello harmonies,

light skin can't hide what ears clearly see
a voice that gullies and steadies your qualms.
white stains my skin and ripples in my hair
bares witness to a father, I dare not love,
each strand a dusty crack cross Race Street*

an eyelash threading a wish, a prayer layered
in cobbled stones to be white, drifting
each face it passes refused to greet.

---

* Race Street was a main street in Cambridge, Maryland, historically
and psychologically divided by race. Whites occupied one side and
Blacks the other.

2.
not a white woman, nor do i wither
in darkness, i bruise a blue rose
blooming between brick i quiver

not a white woman, nor do i wither
my song crawls, my voice slithers
frost bit lips, trill away my woes

not a white woman, nor do I wither
in darkness, i bruise a blue rose

3.
silence.
no song.
beat me. bid—
quiet. gag me.
dead

4.

something has died. there. silence where a song once lived.
iron cuffed neck, wrists. no heaven. no one forgives.

persecute me. an ice water baptism wakes my soul
for refusing. new bossman. first day on patrol.

this warden, Cassidy, wants me to waltz wrong, turned right,
whispering *life is better if crazy and white—*

you solo dance cracks between alabaster tile—
you live in the black—you have gleamed white all the while

5.
black bird, oriole,
can do anything, but sing
alone. she needs sisters
black-winged melodies, the souled
contraltos of dark angels.

BOUND/
DEMARCATION;
BOUNDARIES

Ida B. Wells with her children (1909)

Ida B. Wells

[July 16, 1862–March 25, 1931]

Ida B. Wells was an African American educator, journalist, newspaper editor, suffragist, sociologist, and an early leader in the long civil rights movement. At an early age, she moved with some of her siblings to Memphis. There she found better pay for teachers. All the way up in Chicago, Wells kept us in the know. She documented lynchings by the location of the lost. Wells was a master statistician. She factored in the financial motivations for lynchings.

Frances Willard isn't on the borders of gender and race. Willard is the queen of democracy, a suffragette with a work ethic, a busybody. I told Wells about the dream, and Willard wanted in. Wells and I wonder why Willard didn't speak up about the lowdown on lynching. It could be because Willard wasn't lying next to her Black man as the phone rang forever with threats. I bet Willard didn't shed a tear when the branch holding the noose tight with flesh folded into flames. What cat had her tongue? Why didn't she confess and tell all of London how a Black man is the incubus of all her moral intentions? Why didn't she testify about his work and how his musk was the emollient of all her liberties?

ΛV=C ≈ ♥V>>! (FOR IDA B WELLS BARNETT II)

λv=c ≈ ♥v>>! there are thieves in the temples
c. 1892 = 241 lynched = [torn from wives' arms x rope + tree (fire)]
white supremacy + mob violence

26 states ∝ united = alabama ≥ 22+arkansas ≥ 25+california
≥ 3+florida ≥ 11+georgia ≥ 17+idaho ≥ 8+illinois ≥ 1+kansas
≥ 3+kentucky ≥ 9+louisiana ≥ 29+maryland ≥ 1+mississippi ≥
16+missouri ≥ 6+montana ≥ 4+newyork ≥ 1+northcarolina ≥
5+ohio ≥ 3+southcarolina ≥ 5+tennessee ≥ 28+texas ≥ 15+virginia
≥ 7+westvirginia ≥ 5+wyoming ≥ 9+arizonaterritory ≥ 3+oklahoma
≥ := δ or ∂. λv=c ≈ ♥v>>! there are thieves in the temples 160
Negro±80 "others." 5 women < 2 states over the mason dixon < 1
free?. √ black economic progress ∏ pure gold american racism and
demon possession of frances willard's good "χ-ians."

λv=c ≈ ♥v>>! there are thieves in the temples. A black man___,
Hastings, had the determination of any of the wise men, girding
through the desert night. like a warning star, he was hoisted like
a holiday ham ≠ murdering a white man. dog-eared like pages to
remember, his [(daughter +son) + χ] ≡ lynched beside him. (χ =
decorated w/bullet holes), this is the Σ of them. arms, fingers, noses
(fracked from their faces like sphinxes), nothing left of his loins. no
one to add to his legacy. Σ black economic progress = |lynching-
advent| χ-mas eve.

λv=c ≈ ♥v>>! there are thieves in the temples
c. 1892 = 241 lynched = [torn from wives' arms x rope + tree (fire)]
white supremacy + mob violence

26 states $\propto$ united = alabama $\geq$ 22+arkansas $\geq$ 25+california $\geq$ 3+florida $\geq$ 11+georgia $\geq$ 17+idaho $\geq$ 8+illinois $\geq$ 1+kansas $\geq$ 3+kentucky $\geq$ 9+louisiana $\geq$ 29+maryland $\geq$ 1+mississippi $\geq$ 16+missouri $\geq$ 6+montana $\geq$ 4+newyork $\geq$ 1+northcarolina $\geq$ 5+ohio $\geq$ 3+southcarolina $\geq$ 5+tennessee $\geq$ 28+texas $\geq$ 15+virginia $\geq$ 7+westvirginia $\geq$ 5+wyoming $\geq$ 9+arizonaterritory $\geq$ 3+oklahoma $\geq$:= δ or ∂. $\lambda v{=}c \approx \heartsuit v{>}{>}$! there are thieves in the temples 160 Negro$\pm$80 "others." 5 women < 2 states over the mason dixon < 1 free?. $\sqrt{}$ black economic progress $\bigcap$ pure gold american racism and demon possession of frances willard's good "X-ians."

$\lambda v{=}c \approx \heartsuit v{>}{>}$! there are thieves in the temples. @ 12 yrs, 1 white girl can be a witness = sleep burned from her eyes. she becomes 1~10,000 to see the kickings of the heart. they are tearing the black man____ all apart. @12 yrs, she watches 1 woman apply a single match to her known lover|black man____|. ?black man____?. black man____, who professes innocence. a flame, 1000s of bullets levy bodies/swinging from branches. black economic progress ($-$ $\propto$) american democracy.

λV=C ≈ ♥V>>! THERE ARE THIEVES IN THE TEMPLES

c. 1892 = 241 lynched = [torn from wives' arms x rope + tree (fire)] white supremacy + mob violence

26 states ∝ united = alabama ≥ 22+arkansas ≥ 25+california ≥ 3+florida ≥ 11+georgia ≥ 17+idaho ≥ 8+illinois ≥ 1+kansas ≥ 3+kentucky ≥ 9+louisiana ≥ 29+maryland ≥ 1+mississippi ≥ 16+missouri ≥ 6+montana ≥ 4+newyork ≥ 1+northcarolina ≥ 5+ohio ≥ 3+southcarolina ≥ 5+tennessee ≥ 28+texas ≥ 15+virginia ≥ 7+westvirginia ≥ 5+wyoming ≥ 9+arizonaterritory ≥ 3+oklahoma ≥ := δ or ∂. λv=c ≈ ♥v>>! there are thieves in the temples 160 Negro±80 "others." 5 women < 2 states over the mason dixon < 1 free?. √ black economic progress ⊓ pure gold american racism and demon possession of frances willard's good "χ-ians."

λv=c ≈ ♥v>>! there are thieves in the temples. 1 white father finds <<♥ ⊥ 2 turtle doved daughters brutally dead. He blames a herd of white neighbors, while 1 black man___, 6 towns away, buys $4.50 worth of rings from a jew. < 1 week later, the buying black man___ swings from a tree || his head chimes ⇒for these crimes|| . black economic progress = ∫ visibility (φ=dangerous visibility)

ΛV=C ≈ ♥V>>! (FOR IDA B. WELLS)
TRANSLATION 1

$\lambda v = c \approx$ ♥$v >> !$ there are thieves in the temples
c. 1892 = 241 lynched = [torn from wives' arms x rope + tree (fire)]
white supremacy + mob violence

The speed of light is almost equivalent to love come in a hurry.
There are thieves in the temples.
In the 1862nd year of the of our Lord,
there were 241 lynched
torn from wives' arms and wedding chambers
Multiply that by the rope. Count the trees they strung from
The torches. All of this
done under the armor of white
supremacy
mob violence

λV=C ≈ ♥V>>! (FOR IDA B. WELLS) TRANSLATION 2

c. 1892 = 241 lynched = [torn from wives' arms x rope + tree (fire)]
white supremacy + mob violence
26 states ∝ united = alabama ≥ 22+arkansas ≥ 25+california
≥ 3+florida ≥ 11+georgia ≥ 17+idaho ≥ 8+illinois ≥ 1+kansas
≥ 3+kentucky ≥ 9+louisiana ≥ 29+maryland ≥ 1+mississippi ≥
16+missouri ≥ 6+montana ≥ 4+newyork ≥ 1+northcarolina ≥
5+ohio ≥ 3+southcarolina ≥ 5+tennessee ≥ 28+texas ≥ 15+virginia
≥ 7+westvirginia ≥ 5+wyoming ≥ 9+arizonaterritory ≥ 3+oklahoma
≥ := δ or ∂. λv=c ≈ ♥v>>! there are thieves in the temples 160
Negro±80 "others." 5 women < 2 states over the mason dixon < 1
free?. √ black economic progress ∏ pure gold american racism and
demon possession of frances willard's good "χ-ians."

Calculations
In the 1862nd year of the Christian calendar there
were 241 lynched in over 26 states
more than half of this Union.
They are the collective, equal to
22 or more murders in Alabama
25 or more offed in the State of Arkansas
3 or more in California
11 or more executed in Florida
17 or more in Georgia
some 8 souls, maybe plus some in Idaho
1 or more offing in Illinois
3 or more lynched in the Free State of Kansas
9 or more people murdered in Kentucky
29 or more noosed in Louisiana

1 or more in Maryland
16 or more souls swing in Mississippi
6 or more killed in Missouri
In Montana, 4 or more
At least one in the State of New York
And 5 or more more murders in North Carolina
A trinity or more people in Ohio
South Carolina carried 5 or more
A crown of 28 or more are lynched in Tennessee
Texas follows with 15 or more taken to the trunks of trees
7 or more swing in Virginia while the Star-Spangled Banner bangs
    from the bay
5 or more people pulled from the neck in Wyoming
9 or more offed from Arizona territory
And another trinity humming something holy moments before they
    are riddled with bullets and sway in the wind.

ΛV=C ≈ ♥V>>! (FOR IDA B. WELLS)
TRANSLATION 3

$:= \delta$

What I tell you is fact and the distribution of the lynching is high and the invisibility of Black people does not equate to zero Black people. We all know that "no" is never really a zero and that zero in context of human life is not a balance number but the sum of a loss—it's a probability measure.

ΛV=C ≈ ♥V>>! (FOR IDA B. WELLS)
TRANSLATION 4

The Queen of Democracy Would Have Elected Trump
The speed of light is almost equivalent to love
come in a hurry. There are thieves
in the temples. 160 Negro bodies
gained in lynchings and stolen from their families.
Those loved ones. 80 others found the same fate. There were
at least five murdered, two states above
the Mason Dixon. At least one state claimed
to be a free one, factored into democracy.
Give the reasons, Why would 54%
white women did not question.
The square root of Black economic progress is the product of all
values. That is to say pure gold American racism. The demon
possession of Frances Willard's good Christians

λV=C ≈ ♥V>>! (FOR IDA B. WELLS)
TRANSLATION 5

$λv=c ≈ ♥v>>!$ there are thieves in the temples. A black man___,
Hastings, had the determination of any of the wise men, girding
through the desert night. like a warning star, he was hoisted like a
holiday ham ≠ murdering a white man. dog-eared like pages to
remember, his [(daughter +son) + χ] ≡ lynched beside him. (χ =
decorated w/bullet holes), this is the Σ of them. arms, fingers, noses
(fracked from their faces like sphinxes), nothing left of his loins. no
one to add to his legacy. Σ black economic progress = |lynching-
advent| χ-mas eve.

Haste
The speed of light is almost equivalent to love come in a hurry.
There are thieves in the temples.
A Black man, name Hastings, had
the determination of any of the wise men
girding through the night.
He was lifted,
hoisted like a holiday ham. To some,
this is not the same as murdering a white man.
Dog-eared like pages to remember,
his daughter and his son
are lynched beside him.
On Christmas Eve
their bodies are littered with bullet holes.
This is the sum of them
arms, fingers, noses fracked
from their faces like sphinxes,
nothing left at the loins,

no one to add to Hastings' legacy.
The sum of Black economic progress
equals the absolute value of lynching
the negative events of the advent season,
collectively multiplied by Christmas Eve

λV=C ≈ ♥V>>! (FOR IDA B. WELLS)
TRANSLATION 6

λv=c ≈ ♥v>>! there are thieves in the temples. @ 12 yrs, 1 white girl can be a witness = sleep burned from her eyes. she becomes 1~10,000 to see the kickings of the heart. they are tearing the black man___ all apart. @12 yrs, she watches 1 woman apply a single match to her known lover|black man___|. ?black man___?. black man___, who professes innocence. a flame, 1000s of bullets levy bodies/swinging from branches. black economic progress (− ∝) american democracy.

Strike of Midnight
At the Stroke of Midnight
the speed of light is almost equivalent
to love come in a hurry.
There are thieves in the temples.
At 12 years old
one white girl can be a witness.
This means that she can have the sleep burned from her eyes
as she becomes 1 of 10,000 witnesses
to the kickings of the heart,
witness to the tearing of a black man.
At 12 years, old she watches one woman
apply a single match to her lover
an isolated black man.
A Black MAN?
One who professes his innocence.
There is a single flame
and 1000s of bullets
leave his body,
swinging from branches.
Black economic progress,

some reason is negatively
proportioned, unequal in the context
of American Democracy.

Portrait of Zora Neale Hurston (1937)

λV=C ≈ ♥V>>! (FOR IDA B. WELLS)
TRANSLATION 7

λv=c ≈ ♥v>>! there are thieves in the temples. 1 white father finds
<< ♥ ⊥ 2 turtle doved daughters brutally dead. He blames a herd
of white neighbors, while 1 black man___, 6 towns away, buys $4.50
worth of rings from a Jew. < 1 week later, the buying black man___
swings from a tree || his head chimes ⇒for these crimes|| . black
economic progress = ∫ visibility (φ=dangerous visibility)

Rings
The speed of light is almost equivalent
to love come in a hurry.
There are thieves in the temples.
A white father finds there is far less love
lying in right angles.
His daughters are turtle-doved,
brutally murdered in their beds.
He blames a herd of white neighbors,
while one black man
six towns away
buys $4.50 worth of rings from a Jew.
Less than a week later
the black man swings from a tree.
This means his head chimes
for these crimes.
Black economic progress
is an integral part of visibility
in a capitalist economy.
Black economic progress is a golden ratio
and a dangerous radiance.

Zora Neale Hurston

[(1891) 1901–1960]

Zora Neale Hurston, a writer and anthropological researcher, did extensive writing and anthropological research on African American and Indigenous cultures. She was sure to uncover most if not everything. She knew all about Marie Laveau, and hurricanes followed her. She was also a journalist for a number of publications and covered famous trials like the one pertaining to Ruby McCollum. She was a hidden figure. She worked as a librarian/archivist at Patrick Air Force Base in Cocoa Beach, Florida, a.k.a. Cape Canaveral Air Force Station. She aided in putting men into space. I wonder if she had anthropological research on alien life? She aided many political campaigns. Hurston was blackballed and outcast from many writing collectives and research groups because she was outspoken and a woman. She died poor, working as a maid. Alice Walker paid for her gravestone and marked it in case we need to claim the bones. In the height of the eugenics movement, she used her scientific research to validate the humanity and in some cases superiority of African and Indigenous cultures. Although she was accepted to two PhD programs, she was unable to formally enroll. She couldn't find a sponsor for any of her research.

ZORA NEALE HURSTON

Before the Bronx Zoo,
Ota Benga boarded a ship flipping
a fish scale like a coin. The first
shiny thing he'd seen since
his family was murdered.
Leopold's soldier still
carries the finger
of Benga's daughter
in his pocket to ward
away evil. Remember him? The man
in with monkeys. Who can forget
the ways Benga grit his teeth? They
resembled claws. Zora reads
of him caged in the zoo, the same year
her mother becomes a ghost.

Thick with wet memories, Zora
has a hard time keeping still. From
Morgan in Baltimore to Howard
in the District to Barnard near
the Bronx, Benga haunts her. In slide
her rituals: folding the news clippings
in with her lunch, reading the creases,
mysteries draped in her palms.

This odd communion; the cradles of Hell
always take the shape of a woman's
lips. Using a looking glass
made from a martini, Madison Grant
traces Zora's square jaw. When she

whispers about Anne Spenser
and the thespian boarder, Benga,
Grant's throat burns with curiosities.
He considers Zora and all that is
alchemy. Is she the prophecy of stones,
the fire within the dark sciences
he conjures?

*Trinidad-born journalist and activist Claudia Jones
(1915–1964) at the offices of the* West Indian Gazette *(WIG)
at 250 Brixton Road, Brixton, south London, circa 1962.
Jones founded the newspaper in 1958 and was its editor
until her death.*

Claudia Jones

[February 15, 1915–December 24, 1964]

Born in Belmont, Port of Spain, Trinidad, Claudia Vera Cumberbatch was a journalist, poet, essayist, and activist. She migrated to New York City at age nine. Her mother died five years later. At seventeen, Jones contracted tuberculosis and was considerably ill for the rest of her life. Despite the fact that she was brilliant, she was discriminated against in most professional environments because of her race, gender, and immigrant status. By twenty-one, she was engaged in activism. Seeking organizations that aided the Scottsboro Boys, she became a member of the Young Communist League USA. She enjoyed a rewarding career in journalism that included becoming editor of *Negro Affairs Quarterly*. Jones is best known for her research that spanned economics, cultural studies, and labor history, "An End to the Neglect of the Problems of the Negro Woman." Claudia was an elected member in the National Committee of the Communist Party USA (CPUSA). She was later tried and falsely found guilty for violating the McCarran Act. She also spent time at the Federal Reformatory for Women in Alderson, West Virginia, for "un-American activities." This is the same prison where Puerto Rican activist and political prisoner Lolita Lebrón and American activist and political prisoner Assata Shakur were imprisoned. She was scheduled for deportation upon release. Jones's mother country, Trinidad, refused her, because "she would be troublesome." The United Kingdom accepted her on humanitarian grounds; 350 people came to see her off. In the UK Claudia quickly founded the *West Indian Gazette and Afro-Asian Caribbean News* in 1958. She was so revered for her efforts with the Communist Party that she was buried left of Karl Marx in Highgate Cemetery in North London.

CLAUDIA JONES

I think I've seen you left
of everywhere. At dawn
when the golden shaves the dark.
You are a daughter of nations'
seamed, stitched with stars, snarling
stripes into ribbons and make Marx.
This is how you send our spirits
into rings. I think I have seen you
lift in the cyphers of callaloo,
swirling about the Earth.

Trinidad's daughter, justice's
town crier and good good girlfriend
of Amy Ashwood Garvey, you fashioned
a world from a fissure—a wide-rimmed
crescent and welcomed black women.

A nation is built brick by brittle
brick, blood in the mortar. A legacy,
page by scared page. How many
ways did you write women? How
many ways did you right women?

Eartha Kitt sleeping on a bus, May 5, 1962

Eartha Kitt

[January 17, 1927–December 25, 2008]

Born in North, South Carolina, she was conceived as a result of her
mother, a plantation worker, being raped by a rich man's son who
owned the plantation. Kitt danced with the Katherine Dunham Com-
pany from 1943 until 1948. Kitt spoke four languages and sang in seven.
I love her. Orson Welles felt she was a Helen of Troy. She recorded
music and starred in theater productions, film, and television. She was
so revered that she was invited to a White House luncheon where Lady
Bird Johnson asked her about the Vietnam War. Kitt told her the truth,
"the children of America are not rebelling for no reason. They are not
hippies for no reason at all . . . They are rebelling against something . . .
They feel they are going to raise our sons—and I know what it's like,
and you have children of your own, Mrs. Johnson—we raise children
and send them to war." It is reported that Mrs. Johnson burst into
tears. It is true that Kitt was blackballed in the United States and she
was branded as "a sadistic nymphomaniac" by the CIA. After ten years
performing overseas, she returned to Broadway. She slowly regained
prominence in music, television, and movies. In addition to being
an anti-war activist, she was a member of the Women's International
League for Peace and Freedom. Kitt was also an advocate for LGBT
rights. Kitt died from colon cancer on Christmas Day in 2008.

EARTHA KITT

Harlem's dandies "aren't tailored for death or army fatigues."
Blue Black love shimmies in Kitt's throat, torching his Southern soul.
Johnson does his lynching in draft letters, yet questions loyalties.

Harlem's dandies "aren't tailored for death or army fatigues,"
trace symmetry of chain gangs and Saigon's zombie infantries.
Kitt's eyes are a battalion of bullets. Her tongue paroled.

Harlem's dandies "aren't tailored for death or army fatigues."
Blue Black love shimmies in Kitt's throat, torching Johnson's soul.

Sonia Sanchez (1972)

Sonia Sanchez

[September 9, 1934–Continuous Fire]

Born Wilsonia Benita Driver, in Birmingham, Alabama, Sanchez lost her mother when she was only two years old. Her grandmother died when she was six. She moved to Harlem with her father when she was nine. She graduated from Hunter College with a degree in political science. She is a writer, plenty poetry collections, plays, and other writings. Louise Bogan and everyone else knows, she's a *homegirl with a handgrenade*. Sanchez is a mother of three children. She is also an activist. She constantly advocates for peace. At seventy-one, on June 28, 2006, Sonia Sanchez, along with eleven other grandmothers, staged a sit-in protest at a large military recruitment center in Philadelphia. Many of the grandmothers were charged with defiant trespassing and arrested. Sanchez and the other activists disrupted the recruitment station and inspired others to join in the fight for peace and protests against the Iraq War.

THIS GRANNY IS A GANGSTER

Love wears a lanyard laced with
readers. Love is a pair of bifocals, the rims
on the nostrils, nursing pouted lips.
Love is a granny, a woman weaved from Alabama
clay and concrete, one that can fold the names
of your enemies in her tongue. A granny that sets out
a candy dish full of sparkling laxatives for bullies.
Sonia Sanchez has long been a soldier of Love.

She wields protests like wind. At 82,
she marches like she is leading
a second line. Awe at her knees. With her cane
she cracks blessings and calls your nearest kin. She
speaks peace in a cadence of prayers.

The army slithers down Broad Street
wanting weapons guiled from flesh. She
shows the recruiter that "freedom
can't be paid for with my grandchildren's
lives." Her love is strong. It is all knuckles
and knotted. "One, two, three and four. Love
doesn't want your bloody war."

March to honor Sandra Bland and protest deaths of Black women in police custody, Minneapolis, Minnesota (2015)

Sandra Bland

[February 7, 1987–July 12, 2015]

Sandra Bland was twenty-eight years old when she was found hanging in a jail cell in Waller County, Texas. Three days earlier, Bland was pulled over and stopped for a minor traffic violation that resulted in her arrest because she attempted to defend herself. Although her death was initially ruled a suicide, it is a fact that the Texas authorities and FBI determined that the Waller County Jail and the arresting officer failed to follow required policies. In September 2016, Bland's mother settled a wrongful death lawsuit against the county jail and police department for $1,900,000. It is important to note that prior to her arrest, Bland curated and documented her protests of police killings on various social media sites using the hashtag #SandySpeaks. Upon her death, her #SandySpeaks works went viral. They stand as an archive, a record of her courage, intelligence, and activism.

#SANDYSPEAKS IS A CHORAL REFRAIN

It could have been me,
with three degrees creased into the front seats,
bits of the constitution in my veins,
like braille. The declarations tattooed inside
my eyelids. How many times did Sally Hemings
have to hear 'bout them and affirm the tiny ego of
Tom, before he bares himself to his brothers
collecting their boastings, forgiving his debts?

It could have been me,
like Sandy, I would have missed them
dashes in the road. The ways I skirt around
corners under the cover of sun. I fleeing
an interview happy to have
some means, pockets fluffy
with promises.

It could have been me,
listening to gospel, the lilts in my throat
running and a Marlboro fog above
my lips. My car would be all clouds,
a Heaven, shaved with blue and red
lights. It would have been me,
my eyebrows high and voice low,
questioning Encinia about his bidding.

It could have been me, a black woman
the color of Oklahoma clay; a policeman pretending to be
some cowboy. Sandy had been in Texas but
a day. How long had he been hunting for one

like her? Encinia seen this in his mind. It was
the means of forgetting the woman
that refused to love him and the black man
she clinged to. In this vision, he is a rodeo
style hero, Sandy is a rogue rascal. He holds
out his tongue to the shower of coins
and praises. A black woman without a job
owns her dignity. Did his fantasy desire
that too? He mined it out of her back
with his knees. History told him that he could squeeze
gold from black women's wrists with iron cuffs. Is that why
he braided the noose to resemble a lasso?

BOUND √HURDLE; SPRING FORTH

Portrait of Harriet Tubman (1868 or 1869)

Harriet Tubman

[1822–March 10, 1913]

Tubman was born a slave in Dorchester County, Maryland, the Eastern Shore in 1822 near the brackish waters. She was physically abused as a pre-emancipated person. One wound on her head resulted in pain, dizziness, and spells of hypersomnia. She had intense dreams and visions from God. She was a gifted woman, a guide. She was an abolitionist, humanitarian, military strategist and spy during the Civil War, herbalist, and ecologist. It is reported that she liberated hundreds of people, I am sure the count is off. She liberated thousands. They called her Moses. John Brown called her General Tubman. She knew the Bible. The Old Testament best. Those books are filled with geography, liberated/pre-emancipated people and Africa. How could she not love them? She was the first woman to organize and lead the liberation of pre-emancipated people along the Combahee River. And she built a home for "aged and indigent colored people." In the 1890s, Tubman had brain surgery. The doctor sawed open her skull. She refused anesthesia and bit down on the bullet as she had seen Civil War soldiers do during amputations. Tubman died with pneumonia at ninety-one in the home she established, and it was named in her honor.

HARRIET IS HOLY

lick a thumb	hold hands to the wind	what is it about
water/women?	take me, Miz Tubman, in tow	her instructions *make*
my mark	X	a river be
as faithful as	daughter of Eve	"mother of Cain"
her face	a rainbow wonder	her smile,
a collection	of stars/of springs	between water/between women
be—no mysteries	I know of no man	stands
waist deep and wet in	these crossings,	mossy riverbeds
like brail	fold in her feet	this woman kneads
these sweet waters	in her palms,	thousands,
call	her "Moses,"	ask the stars
even Jesus needed	a "John the Baptist"	with arms wide
her	she in the intersections	she be revolver/rescue

bound√hurdle; spring forth 105

Portrait of Joan Little from the Bettye Lane Collection (1978)

Joan Little

[Born in 1953–unknown]

Born and raised in Washington, North Carolina, Joan was the oldest of ten children and was their caregiver until she was able to find work picking tobacco and waitressing. She graduated high school in Philadelphia. Joan spent short times away from North Carolina, but always returned home. She knew how to take things without paying for them. She was arrested many times. On August 27, 1974, she stabbed Clarence Alligood with an icepick in self-defense. Alligood used the icepick to threaten her life as he raped her. Joan maintains that she didn't kill him, she just defended herself in an attempt to stop Alligood from raping her again. Two other women inmates were also his victims. They testified at Joan Little's trial. She was charged with first-degree murder. In a highly publicized trial, Joan Little was found not guilty. The a capella group founded by the freedom singer Bernice Johnson Reagon, Sweet Honey in the Rock, wrote a tribute to her titled "Joanne Little" (1976).

JOAN LITTLE

The wind in Washington County carries.
No one keeps to themselves. Rumors
soil. A caterpillar looks like a worm,
and a worm, like a snake; fact is
everything that crawls ain't looking
to be a butterfly. But, why
take a garden rake to a bird? It's no
secret, cops welcome a reason
to kill anything. Ask the people
they cage.

Only crows bred in captivity collect
things. Corvids, they say—nature's
compulsive hoarders. What
is a jeweled ring in the beak
of a thief? A confession. What
they come to call a horde of crows?
A murder. We are not the only ones .
to speak over our dead. How she carried on
at her window, feeding the fowl first.
This kept guards in stitches.

In the light of day, one jailer
rakes the rails of her cell until they bleed
mercy on the edge of his icepick. The one
he stores in the desk. Even when she caws,
he enters. A man ever reach his dick for you?
Between the bars, his hand forcing
his worm forward, you running backwards, waving
no, your fingers loose like laces, barricading

what you see as precious? His whispers
scrape the curves of Joan's
crooked beak. His semen, a stain
lifting each of her feathers.

Will Ruby's Baby Become A 'New' Legal Landmark?

By WILLIAM BRADFORD HUIE

As a final development in the case of Ruby McCollum, the little three-year-old girl pictured here may become the most famous child ever born to a Negro mother and a white father.

She may become a legal landmark, like Dred Scott, in the progress of the Negro in America from slavery to responsible, first-class citizenship.

For to her may go the distinction of being the FIRST mulatto child ever to be recognized by a Supreme Court in a Southern state as the LEGAL, as well as the natural, heir of a white father.

Here is how this may develop:

The child's first name is Loretta. Her mother is Ruby Jackson McCollum, now held in the Florida State Hospital for the Insane as the murderess of the child's father, Dr. Clifford LeRoy Adams, of Live Oak, Suwannee County, Florida.

* * *

RUBY, WITHOUT question, is a Negro, believed to have no white blood in her ancestry.

When she killed the doctor on Aug. 3, 1952, she had for twenty years been the wife of Sam Mc-Collum, also a full-blooded Negro. Ruby and Sam had three full-blooded Negro children, and Sam died the day after the murder.

The child, Loretta, had been born ten months prior to the murder, and she, under Florida law, is a mulatto, which, strictly speaking, is the first-generation offspring of a pure Negro and a white.

So what now is Loretta's last name? Is it Loretta McCollum? Or Loretta Jackson? Or Loretta Adams?

* * *

Both of Loretta's "fathers"— both Sam McCollum and LeRoy Adams — are dead. Both of them left estates without wills. So which "father" should Loretta inherit from?

* * *

ALMOST A year ago, when I began digging into the State of Florida v. Ruby McCollum, Ruby, of course, was under death sentence and on the way to the electric chair.

The State of Florida contended, in effect, that Loretta's father was Loretta McCollum, and that her natural as well as legal father was Sam McCollum. The State of Florida, in demanding the death penalty, had branded as "preposterous" Ruby's claim that Doctor Adams was Loretta's natural father.

Moreover, the State of Florida, in the person of Suwannee County Judge J. M. Hearn, is custodian of the $140,000 estate of the late Sam McCollum.

And the state officially recognizes five heirs: Ruby, Loretta, and the other three children. Each of the four children is to receive one-fifth of the estate as he comes of age.

* * *

RUBY IS a legal pauper. Her one-fifth of Sam's estate is "gone," because lawyers hold $18,000 in assignments against it, and Florrie Lee Adams, white widow of the doctor, holds

father of Loretta. But can I also prove that he is the legal father, and that the child has the right to inherit from his estate?

I believe I can—and my attorneys believe there is an excellent chance. The question the law asks is: Did the father acknowledge the child? Is the acknowledgement in writing? Is the acknowledgement firmly established?

I believe I possess all the evidence that is necessary. As what is known legally as the "Next Friend" of the child, I hope soon to bring an action in the Florida courts which will establish Loretta as the legal heir of her white father, LeRoy Adams.

SINCE DOCTOR Adams now has two heirs, a white daughter and the white widow, the action will claim for Loretta a third of whatever estate Doctor Adams left.

* * *

THE CAREFUL reader will now have to understand what is meant by these words natural and legal.

The laws regarding paternity and bastardy in the United States are a national disgrace, even where all parties are legally white.

And where some of the parties are not legally white, there either are no laws at all or the situation is one of medieval cruelty.

* * *

Even in all-white relationships, a child can be the natural child of a man without being the legal child. You can prove that a man is a natural father and still not be able to prove that he is a legal father.

In short, you can sire a child, and you can prove that he is the sire; but you still may not be able to prove that the offspring has the legal right to inherit from the father.

* * *

SO IN FLORIDA I am now in this position: I can prove, beyond doubt, that LeRoy Adams was and is the natural

denied the right to inherit from Sam McCollum, should she not then inherit from LeRoy Adams?

One point, of course, gives me concern. Do I have the right to jeopardize the child's present inheritance?

If no action is taken, the child will get money from the Sam McCollum estate for her rearing and her education.

BUT SUPPOSE I take—or encourage—an action which cuts the child off from the McCollum estate, and then the effort fails to establish her as an Adams heir?

These are problems which one encounters in the strange maze of laws which govern our mores. But of this I am certain.

If the Florida Supreme Court should one day announce the right of Loretta What's-Her-Name to inherit from the estate of the late State Senator-elect Clifford LeRoy Adams, then little Loretta will have struck a blow for humanity that will be heard around the world.

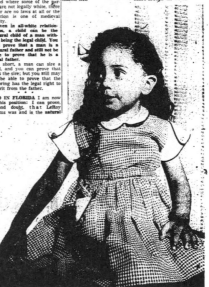

Page 21 of the Pittsburgh Courier, *December 4, 1954*

Ruby McCollum

[August 31, 1909–May 23, 1992]

Ruby McCollum was born Ruby Jackson on August 31, 1909, in Zuber, Florida. At the age of twenty-two, she married Sam McCollum and the couple moved to Nyack, New York. The couple moved back to Florida in 1934 with their son Sam Jr. After sharing a home and business with Sam's brother Buck McCollum, Sam and Ruby move to Live Oak, Florida. In Live Oak, they own a funeral home and a string of business, some illegal, all lucrative. The town doctor, C. LeRoy Adams, wants part of the business. The McCollums meet his monetary demands. Later the doctor wants Ruby, wife of Sam and mother of three children. He is from a southern family and thinks she is his right, a paramour, a white man's pleasure, a Black mistress of his choosing to bear his children. Dr. C. LeRoy Adams is soon elected senator. He is busy, but he still finds the time to father Ruby McCollum's fourth child. He may have fathered her fifth child if Ruby hadn't shot him and ended the relationship on August 3, 1952. We will not know. She was not allowed to testify during her trial. She was convicted of murder and later declared crazy.

Zora Neale Hurston, a writer and anthropological scientist, has done extensive research on paramour rights in the timber mills of Northern Florida. She covers Ruby's trial for the *Pittsburgh Courier* before the newspaper stops paying for Zora's reports. Despite this, Hurston writes about McCollum after her conviction. Hurston also revisits some of the particulars of McCollum's case in a short story titled "The Conscience of the Court" for the *Saturday Evening Post*. Solidarity stokes a strong pen.

RUBY McCOLLUM

They lie. Some say that Ruby and her
husband, Sam, are Live Oak's Black Bonnie
and Clyde, but make no mention of her fine house
with a pool and the ring of policemen swimming
in her and Sam's pockets.

I swear, between Alabama and the Gulf, it's hard
to keep anything out of a gator's mouth, out
of a raccoon's grip. Some bandits are dirty
as the Devil, crawling into the yard reaching . . .

Greedy bandits treat an open window
as an invitation. You can find them fat and splayed,
sultan kings crisscrossed in your satins. They reach,
clawing you close, whispering "paramour," threatening
to tear any black man to pieces. These are the ways, he
is going to disrobe you, fit you to bear his rascals.

A raccoon never retreats, not for threat of bait
or broom. They will run you ragged, race.
Ever wake to find yourself prostrate
Dr. Adams' floor, dressed for church,
praying for a prescription or some poison? Ruby
needed a bit of something to rid her of the little
rascal scratching inside. No? Who else
would she call when a critter insists on living
within her walls?

Grace Jones (2018)

Grace Jones

[May 19, 1948–Still shaming uninspiring pop stars all around the globe]

Grace Jones was born in Spanish Town, St. Catherine, Jamaica, into a religious Pentecostal family. She was raised by her grandparents until she was about thirteen and then she moved to Syracuse, New York, with her parents and continued to practice the faith.

Despite being bullied for her looks as a child, Jones began her career as a fashion model. In 1977, she secured a recording deal with Island Records. She began making dance, new wave, and reggae music. Her music video collection *A One Man Show* is Grammy Award–winning. She largely influenced the cross-dressing movement of the 1900s. The various ways that Jones expressed gender and beauty in her fashion choices continues to inspire many. She cannot be boxed in. She will change and become new again.

AMAZING GRACE AND UNLOVED GENTILES

Your life is one of acrobatics

    and adaptation. Wearing a tilted hat

on the runway, one side white

    with fright. The other side soiled deep

with pleasure. Glamour is picking your teeth

    with a glittered peacock feather.

Security is knowing your stiletto

    —an axe extending from your hips.

Power pulses through your knees.

    Thrust them. Your nose in the straights

Make God call your name

    with curiosity. Make Aphrodite evil.

Make her believe that you are

    the second coming. Make father forget

daughter, enchant, emblazon, transfix—

    your face of stone, a religion. Pay avannij

disciples. Make Adonis hate you. Let everyone

    know that Cupid is your crybaby, jealous,

with rage. Make Orpheus turn,

    his beautiful boys crawl—

between your hips out of thick

    curiosities. Wear your brother's suits

until he casts all mirrors into the garden.

    Spit shards of glass into his ribs. Consecrate

your genitals in your hands. They . . .

    unloved Gentiles.

Fannie Lou Hamer (1964)

Fannie Lou Hamer

[October 6, 1917–March 14, 1977]

Fannie Lou Hamer was born Fannie Lou Townsend, the youngest of her parents' twenty children. Hamer started picking cotton with her family at age six. By age thirteen she picked like a grown person, two to three hundred pounds a day. She married "Pap" Hamer. They worked on the plantation for eighteen years. Hamer went in to have surgery for a tumor and came out without her uterus. This type of medical violation of Black women is common. The civil rights struggle was a deeply spiritual one. She was a crier, a caller, a blues woman of the ethical persuasion with righteous content in The Movement. She was fired from her sharecropping job because she attempted to register to vote. Two women were murdered that same night by whites who believed the two women may have been Ms. Hamer. In Winona, Mississippi, she was falsely accused, arrested, beaten, and raped. It took her months to physically and psychologically recover. She returned as an organizer for the voter registration drives and other civil rights activities. She mentored student activists Sammy Younge Jr. and Wendell Paris. Her testimony about the intersectional oppression and the pervasiveness of white supremacy was so poignant, President Lyndon B. Johnson feared airing it on television. In 1972, Hamer was elected as a Democratic national party delegate. She died of hypertension and breast cancer on March 14, 1977.

MAGNOLIA'S STATE
(FOR FANNIE LOU HAMER)

All the pretty little horses
pluck the kernels from the puffs
like fine plumes. Patch the children's
pockets with collards. *Pick a bail of*
cotton. Tell the story of Emmett
Till. *Keep your lamp trimmed*
and burning. Name every chicken
that flew the coop for a woman
you love. Prove you are literate.
Volunteer and vote. *Certainly Lord,*
your worthless crop-keeping cousin,
parades in white. He will fire
at you. When he takes your job, he will
want your life. You will sing *I'm going*
down to the River of Jordan.

I'm gonna land on the shore.
Woke up this morning knowing
the only thing left to be
is free. *Amazing grace* is a Mississippi Melody,
a ballad like Bessie Smith
marching down Jericho.
Your song
bellowing in the blood.

BOUND—HEM;
HEMMED IN

(FOR ASSATA SHAKUR)

Trenton, N.J.: Reputed black militant leader Joanne Chesimard laughs as she is escorted from federal court in Trenton, New Jersey, April 20, 1977. Miss Chesimard is serving a life sentence for the 1973 murder of a New Jersey state trooper and came to court to request a transfer to a minimum security prison.

Assata Shakur

[July 16, 1947]

Assata Shakur was born JoAnne Deborah Byron in Jamaica, Queens, New York City, where she lived with her grandparents. After her parents divorced, she lived in the coastal town of Wilmington, North Carolina, with her grandmother. Her Aunt Evelyn was her hero. She encouraged her to read, exposed her to new things, and took her to museums and the theater. Assata went to the Borough of Manhattan Community College in order to get a certification to improve her employment situation. She began to read history. She began to understand the complexities of America and how those complexities were embedded in the freedom struggles of Black people, particularly women. The FBI became very interested in her. After graduation, Shakur became involved in the Black Panther Party. She left due to the struggles pertaining to gender roles. There were a number of charges brought against her; she was acquitted of most. On May 2, 1973, she and two friends were pulled over by New Jersey state troopers. The stop resulted in multiple shootings and the death of Zayd Shakur and Werner Foerster. Assata was shot in the shoulder while holding up her hands. Assata was convicted in 1977 and imprisoned in several maximum-security prisons. Assata escaped prison in 1979. She is a descendant of marooned Black people. When the FBI posted wanted posters for Assata, community members posted "Assata Shakur is Welcome Here" posters in response. After several years, Shakur sought and was granted political asylum in Cuba, where she continues to be engaged in activism.

REVOLUTION: ASSATA IN 1956

Revolution ain't a date in a history book,
it's an ivy that thorns,
a lily that pricks. It stings
like the splash of a copper-colored girl
running in a skinned knee,
ruining her Easter dress.

Revolution is the taste of honey
and the revenge of the hive.
Who has the time to watch
swarms die. Revolution ain't got a thang
to do with facts. It is all faith!
Revolution is not a sweet-tooth craving;
it is a long fight clouded in fear; it is
hundreds of hornets. It is family
hunting you.

Revolution is something
that follows. It's a relative
that wrings you 'round the elbow,
a human leash to snatch you
from dreaming. The last time
I saw revolution, she was being dragged
the faces of her toes were screaming.

Revolution ain't a promise you remember,
it's a shriek that damns.
It's the sand gripping your hair,

It is sand brushed into your eyes.

Revolution is jumping into the ocean
with your eyes open, because
you are never sure if bees
can swim. Revolution is drowning
in chiffon. Revolution
is the silk that wouldn't stay out
of your nostrils. Revolution is what
wouldn't be weighted down or let
you go unless you left
the water.

Revolution is the dazzle of the beads
and the buckles of your shoes, collecting salt
beneath the waves. It is choking,
It is the lace snagging from your socks,
and your hair bows snaked across the
neighbors' lawn. Revolution is
what shames the weary biding
grace; they are the welt waiting to redeem
you, the weal waiting for you
in a loved one's grip.

RETINA: ASSATA IN 1970

My eyes are rummaging. This is
a recitation on revolution. A chant

that makes lace of the treetops. My
neighbor in Ferguson wears bifocals

and says that all black folks look alike
at the end of a sniper's lens and how

it's been this way since the great wars.
Does monochromacy make it

easier to see green? Wilderness is such
a good steal for the money. When

you refuse to own land that was not loaned to
you from the First Nations, they paint

you all shades of bandit and thief. Stain
your granny's eyes glass. Your family

watches for your footsteps like spoons
syncopating across the knees. We know

you travel in the spirituals. We are
praying for your safety.

EVERY BLACK WOMAN KNOWS
THE CONSTITUTION: ASSATA IN 1972

You should have carried a shotgun, just
inside the arm, hemmed from pit to hip,

bell-bottom pants and ballooned sleeves. If
you followed Ida B. Wells' instructions,

you wouldn't wear that hole in your
shoulder. The one that can't stand

being nursed or the grazing
of a bra strap. The spirit of

the grandmother is born through
the body of the mother. You

are a woman that chases fear. Hugging it
from the back. Happiness is not

a reward with its salty
hide of tolerance. You,

African Gypsy, two-stepping
when presenting arms. Your joy

is a belt spanning the barrelhouse
blues.

bound—hem; hemmed in   131

TRUTH IS A MIRROR IN THE HANDS OF GOD: ASSATA IN 1976

For true, from the long end
of the looking glass, it appears

isolation is one way to quell
a revolution. What of the mushrooms

and the cilium, the soft bridge of quills
along your lips, the coils of stalactite

forming at your chin? Each with her own
complaints under the waves. Women warriors

are scattered around the world with mouths
men consider wounds and rivers

in their veins. Do you know Marie Laveau?
She had a black liberation community

and a bevy of lwa, she held like rosaries, until each
rinsed through her fingers. St. John's Eve carries

fires from every pillar and post. In her
song, she layered the whistles of water

and wind, a lullaby for the flames. Her pipe
stuffed with fennel and elderflower. Her pockets

bulging with rosemary and lemon verbena,
the summer solstice on her shoulders. I bet

you could mistake her for a mirror?

EXODUS: ASSATA IN 1979

Nothing whole can be ground, grain
or otherwise, fairytale about the new

geographies. What of bondage
is birthright? Is conditioning.

In a Spaniard's tongue, your American mother
twisted the locks of a segregated

amusement park. She possessed
the power of the Pentecost. Did you

inherit the shibboleth of the believers? When
has God ever sent bread? Heaven sent

women with downs of manna. Lava coats
their tongues. Your jaw is a cornerstone

engraved in the guards' punches. You
have nothing to confess. Fists are

the only fruits. They want
to hear you sob their scriptures.

THE EDUCATION OF THE *TAW* MARBLE:
ASSATA A TIMELESS LESSON
IN GEOGRAPHY AND GEOMETRY

Women *elephant stomp* this earth
until they are scattered about

the dust. Isolation is one way to wrestle
resistance. Alone. Two armed guards

think you are a *duck*, they fuss
about your wings. Is *Paradise Lost*

Milton's account of revolution told through
the *devil's eye*, splinted between a tin bit

and the covers of a book? You are swelling.
The walls and the ceilings become braille.

Your blood makes the floor a gossip,
snitching on the weak architecture of this cell.

Your eyes leak salt. What is left of regret,
the dirge of spilled milk? And then

it hits you. Escaping is as easy as any game
of marbles. Faith is the mind's first arithmetic.

Your memory gushes. You are
a descendent of Cimarrons, people

who know geography is only one theory
of relativity, a matter of geometry, a numbers

story. *Knuckle down* in the creek
and bolt for the swamps.

Assata Taught Me

A RECKONING: ASSATA IN 1980

Despite the fact that the new world's
maps are carved out of the ebony

underbellies of Africans, you
grew into a "Moses"

woman, a Harriet Tubman, standing
between the ocean sprays

and morning stars. Thumbtacks crown
your wanted posters. I envision you

a savior born on western soil, a second
coming, another Jonah, the cargo inside,

some bit of contraband, a sharp
gallstone in the bile of Ahab's whale.

SPACE PROGRAM: ASSATA IN 1981

The speckled patterns of the space
program are the ornaments of war's

ephod. Are the hunger pains and ignorance
of children mistaken for chimes? Is

The Cold War over: have they called
a draw? Brittle from all the ways it has been

touched, your intake photo may be
the guidon of miracles. It seems

God is busy. You disappeared
like the Jew, Elijah, a black woman

emancipated by the wind, like a pumpkin
seed dancing in a prayer. Under the canopy

of your name, everything is green's first gold.
You are more beautiful than your enemies,

remember.

THE ARMS RACE/THE WAR ON DRUGS:
ASSATA IN 1984

Ronald Reagan never converted. He remained
an actor. He grinned, said the arms race

was over and pushed a wooden nickel into public school
lunch programs. Desperate to caress

the sweat of the rainbow, he huffed his knuckles
in the clay, a wish for your power.

Your aura is a prism, a space where colors refract
and bow, obliging your every gesture. He can't

forget it. You do the impossible, weave
unity in the bands of a crescent. You are his

obsession, a black mark of beauty
on his neck he calls a cancer,

a spade in his eye, an uncalculated risk,
splendor glowing beyond streetlights. With

your dreadlocks thick and course in the voices
of children, he will make filaments

from your hair. *America's Most Wanted.*
He musters up a murder, a reason

to negotiate. He scales solidarity against
your life, divides it by the national debt.

Your image becomes the subject
of satellites, worshiped by every star.

Each looms like a lotus flower in your lap.

BOUND ∞HINGE

Protest against the deaths of Black women in police custody,
Minneapolis, Minnesota (2015)

Gynnya McMillen

Gynnya McMillen is among a growing number of young girls that are being detained across the country for misdemeanor crimes. On January 11, 2016, seventeen hours after she was booked in a Kentucky juvenile detention center, she was found dead. McMillen refused to remove her sweatshirt in order to be searched. She was placed in an Aikido Control Technique restraint, a martial arts move used to strangle people. In an effort to remove her sweatshirt?

TRAINERS FOR GYNNYA McMILLEN

Danger is beauty. Training
wheels are mystical, lopsided
and long-ways, they carry a body
rickety ways round the 'bouts. Her bike
is a bit too tiny, training bras proved
useless.

She wears oversized sweatshirts.
Her anger makes hot air balloons.
They hide her bloom. In juvie,
they treat privacy like a penalty. The
leather flippers of guardmen grab,
searching her for shrapnel and the serrated
edges of underwire. They take her soul,
no cell of hers is spared. She tucks
her heart into the sleeve of her wrists.
All is pinched between cuffs.

"Patriot and Prisoner" demonstrates the tensions I feel between my allegiance to the United States government and my commitment as a mother. It discusses my experiences serving in the United States Air Force and contrasts them with my experiences as a mother of a Black man and potentially a target of police brutality.

PATRIOT AND PRISONER

(an ode to The One-Legged Stool)

You didn't see that. I wasn't curled up like a baby, officer. You did not see me shit in the corner of this cell. Would you just drag me out of solitary and then put a bullet through my brains or worse for nothing? You call that justice? I ain't do shit. I didn't rip pages from the Bible and make cigarillos. I didn't take nothing from fucking nobody. You got it on video. Look! I've been kneeling here running my fingers across this concrete wishing for water. You didn't see me dip my finger in my own urine and draw it to my nose. You didn't see it. You mind your goddamn business. My pee smell like Arizona Iced Tea. My tightly rolled locks keep falling from my afro in clumps. They taste like Skittles. Don't you know I'll never . . . No, don't care what you whisper into the darkness of this cage, making me believe it came out of my own head. I won't believe a word. Lies, lies, lies. You're lying. Those state officials ain't say what you said they said. They ain't laughing at them protests and memorials. They ain't dropping those charges against your black-blooded blue brothers. I ain't cooperating in crippling democracy. They ain't talking to Senator Kamala Harris like that, like she ain't a child of God. Lies. Lies. Lies. It ain't the way you say it is. I am American. I mean, I mean if I, if we were not here and you on the other side of the door. Like if you were in the neighborhood, I mean, I mean, would you shoot me on the lawn before I could ask you to take me to the hospital? Maxine Waters, she ain't stop side-eye/evil-eyeing the president like you say. Lies. How many times are you trying to kill me? Twice, three times, four, how many? You can't break me. You ain't see me sweat. I wasn't ever worried 'bout your bullshit. You never saw my fists folded around my neck. The hand is quicker than the eye. The hand is quicker than the eyes. You ain't see my hands around my neck. You didn't hear me whisper "I can't breathe, I can't breathe" You ain't heard me, or did you? (laughing) I'm laughing at you. I'm laughing at you. You think I'm the trouble coming your way? Oh, yeah? What you say? You pig, you 5-0, you po-po, you para-military, you not really real, you crooked cock cop! That's right I can get nasty too! You want me to be nasty? You want me to be your little hot pot of bubbling brown sugar? You looking at me, Blue Badge Daddy? Looking in on me like you some raven and I am some morsel of soft and slick in the soil. You don't know shit. I can give the devil Hell! I am God's most beloved. I can take my life right now and be in Heaven the next minute . . . I am the mind-blowing miracle America made me, a womb-wearing trickster. Looka here. Looka here. (seductively) You know I make love to two-ton cluster bombs? I rodeo ride 'em, baby. When I do, I call the name of every incendiary bullet like it's an infidel's child. I nibble at 'em. I use my teeth to engrave initials on the bullets. Oh, you don't believe me? You ain't see that? You ain't see that. The water in my eye. You'll find them initials right under USA—when you find the bodies. Americans, we so good at making a mess disappear in a bigger one. The way we spray Agent Orange and burn lakes of crude oil, I mean those lakes eat flesh, but the bullets . . . they stay and it was my job to put some baby's name on each one. (coy) I know how to walk out of a nightmare backwards, baby, switching the whole while. Anything to grind a mind to dust? Who you looking at? You ain't see me shitting in the corner. I was over there showing you the wide rim of a golden goblet, the one sitting square between my hips. Stop looking at me. Stop looking at me. What you think? You think I'm scared of you? You wanna see me squirm? You think you showing me how your band of brothers killing somebody else's child is gonna somehow hurt me? Break me? (laughing) You don't see me. You can't hurt me. I been a warrior. You know who you looking at? You know who the fuck you looking at? My ancestors been here since before the first American revolution. I am a third-generation veteran. And what the police force paying you? Enough to afford you a flip phone? Oh, I know they say just enough to keep you standing here all day gazing in on me. Yeah that is how it works. Keep the work dangerous, wages low. You know who you looking at? You don't know who the fuck you looking at? (Laughing) You don't who the fuck you looking at. The Department of Defense know me. Know my granddaddy, he helped them first pilots see through stone. He is a yellah Black man, but they call him "infer-red." He ain't like me. I am like my granddad's grandfather—marooned. What the fuck are you looking at? What you like my clothes? My perfume? In the '90s, them recruiters smell me coming, static electricity and ashes. I tell them I'm all-star shine and clay, but they stupid like you and don't know the difference. All they know is the name. They know it's worth the cash to set me in a can box of missiles and bombs. I mean technology and weapons, right? They rivet in my blood. Who you think you looking at? You better call that number. Name, rank—Senior Airman D. H___. Serial number 333-kiss my ass. (runs up the window and smacks it) Who you calling a wench? Use my name. Matter of fact, you ain't got the security clearance to know my fucking name. Make an utterance, make an utterance, any reference to me . . . see if your people don't throw you in with the black lot and ignore your existence. What you think? You think I'm scared of you? You wanna see me squirm? You think you showing me how your band of brothers killing somebody else's child is gonna somehow hurt me? Break me? (laughing) You like me? You like me, blue daddy? I look pretty to you? I could be your Black baby? (coy) All this powder on my face, it ain't goddess paint. I been standing next to my son. He dusts BB bullets with cocaine. He got my soft eyes. You see, he takes the gun straight to his nostril every 23 minutes. He been high ever since Trayvon died. See, he walks in-and-out of stores and after football games in the streets, because those roads swell with drunk white kids and he don't like to be called no nigger, so he walks in the middles on the yellow line and he is hyped on coke because he wants to stay awake—

forever—because all this mess done drove sleep from his soft eyes and the images of Mike Brown's dead body done stayed. (blows a kiss from her palm) You want to kiss my face? Soldier/officer? Come here, blue daddy, come give me a kiss? Give mama some sugar? You don't want some of this delicious? Remember how your granddaddy said all the good flesh been wasting ever since Black folks left the field. He meant his bed, but it don't matter when your dick is pulsing in my palms, your eye sockets will be emptied. You can't see me.

COPING

1. To manage your son's addiction, you must pick at your cuticles day and night until the silos of skin float in your sheets.

2. You will pick them until pus seals the sheets. They will begin to hold you in. They will provide little comfort and fail. You are splintering under the weights of worries.

3. You will leave him voicemails promising to hold him like he is an infant.

4. You will keep a call list of every jail, because you refuse to call the morgues. You will memorize this list until it is the sickle in your eyes. This way you cannot envision his emaciated limbs or consider all the ways his vomit sticks to him, how it is all scaled into his face.

5. After this, you pray he isn't dead.

6. You want something like justice, this desire grows in you like an addiction.

7. You wish that you were a holy virgin mother and he knew that he was God's son and had the power to float like Elijah above his powders and abandon the stairs of his delusions.

A pregnant DaMaris Hill (April 1994)

A RECIPE FOR A SON

In a woman whose skin tastes of honey, mold
brown sugar and molasses. Sift in courage
siphoned from poplar tree ashes. Set aside
the angel's plumes. They will be set to his
back and diamonds,
the stars in his eyes.

a son golden like fresh harvested grains,
each a kernel cradled with compassion. Add
granules of conceit. The palate will
welcome the musky
taste of truffle and name him noble.

Forty weeks, pray him resilient. Pray
brilliance never bronzes. Make him forget
he is mortal. Name him for the gods. Make him
believe. He is the miracle spun
from an oracle's mumbling hand.

GABRIEL CASTS A KNUCKLE

My son has always been fond of grand

gestures. He admires the ways
of the dandy angel Gabriel.

When my son blows his horn

to signal that we are war against one
another, I weep for him. He doesn't

know he was birthed of a Phoenix. He

doesn't know how many times I tasted
my own ashes or licked my lava wounds gilded.

He sees weak and wrinkled. He is blind

to the ways time traces my face
with histories. He is too young to know

the measures, how he entered the earth

surfing the thick membranes of my pain. I
pushed his-side of myself through three quarters

of the way through a window and held him

there to keep his eyes from bursting into pulp.
The plaster of my womb has always been

a potion the devil fears. My son

warns me about his anger; I smile
tasting the gusts he blows. He has begun

dismissing me with his hands. I catch his knuckle
in my lip. He is a child of privilege and clueless

to the ways my teeth shave
ostrich shells. He wasn't there when I dragged

my feet across the waters before creation.
His unancient ears are deaf to my melodies.

He doesn't recognize this poet's libretto,
the nuanced ways I call everything into

being. He is mistaken. My seven-rayed
nimbus is not a halo or a lesser crown.

REMAINS

He was born from the bruised side

of a golden dung beetle.
His tongue gouges toward me, I glare
into his coal eyes for the reflection of
my peacock feathers. I remind him that teal,
purple, and brass are radiant. Eternal.
My flamed wings fan
him cool amid his infant cues.

Fire is the amber jewel
in these lessons. I want to die

just once with him in my arms. Show him
Hell in order to gift him the secrets of
resurrection. Show him that all soot
isn't bitter. Instruct him. Show him how tears
can be transformed into poisons, wet embers
fury's gold.

PRAYING FOR SONS

It is never as easy as some believe,
praying "I have but one son." God answers,
"as did the Father Abraham. And what of me?
I gave my only son for love."

Cupping my insolence into words
I ask God if her son's face was beautiful,
something star blended and bright as Lucifer? I ask
her were there diamonds in her son's eyes? "Did
the rest of him glisten like cobalt beneath a curtain
of night?"

She answers, "Every son is the star he chooses.
Some sons choose to be men, hatch from womb
wanting the world and all its lusts. Other sons
want the heavens. Envy swells in their veins,
jealousy pools in their mouths. It throbs in them.
They will throw their crowns into the clouds. They
aim to collect your sun."

ACKNOWLEDGMENTS

I am grateful to the editors from the Project on the History of Black Writing; Mammoth Publications; *African American Review*; *Reverie: Midwest African American Literature*; *The Black Bottom: An African American Blog of Politics, Culture, and Social Activism*; *Kweli Journal*; *Meridians: Feminism, Race, Transnationalism*; *Crab Orchard Review*, *The Pierian Literary Journal*, *Furious Flower: Seeding the Future of African American Poetry*; *The Offing*; "Prison Industrial Complex and Capital Punishment," a special issue of *Tidal Basin Review*; and *Musiqology* for publishing early drafts of these poems.

I am also grateful for the institutional support of Project on the History of Black Writing, the University of Kansas, the University of Kentucky, the Key West Literary Seminar and Workshop, the Sentencing Project, Eckerd College Writers' Conference: Writers in Paradise, Callaloo Creative Writing Workshop, the Latino Writers Collective, Conjure Woman Writers Conference in Poetry at Chicago State University, the Paden Institute, the Center for Black Literature at Medgar Evers College, CUNY and SUNY Plattsburgh, the New Hampshire Writers' Project, the Kentucky Foundation for Women, the Watering Hole, the Vermont Studio Center, Urban Bush Women, Bread Loaf Writers' Conference, the CityLit Project, the MacDowell Colony, and the generous support of the Furious Flower Poetry Center. Without the patronage and safe harbor of these institutions, this manuscript may have been further delayed.

Special thanks to my editor, Nancy Miller, editor in chief at Bloomsbury Publishing USA, for sharing my vision and investing in my work. Charlotte Sheedy, thank you for so many things, particularly the ways you nurtured my writer-self and all her prickly parts. Ally Sheedy, thank you for encouraging me to fan my feathers and stud my thorns in ink.

Thank you to all of my partners in this writing life, my FirstDays, Tribe, Pencil Shout, Wintergreen Women, Tidal Basin family, and others. I am also grateful to Kali N. Gross and Deb Willis. Their brilliance served as a form of ekphrasis. I am ever grateful to my peers and loved ones who first laid eyes on these poems, like Denise Low, Joanne Gabbin, Howard Rambsy, Kenton Rambsy, Nikky Finney, Chris Abani, Natasha Tretheway, Meta DuEwa Jones, and Monifa Love Asante. In addition, this book would have not been possible without the love and support of my family and friends—far too many to name. Thank you for your encouragement, shelter, and sustenance. To my nephews and nieces, may you be boundless. To my son, spring forth!

I am very thankful to my ancestors, blood relatives or otherwise, for this time and space. I am also grateful for their guidance and permission. I am grateful to God for all things. May this book live.

CITATIONS

"Tearful Joan Little Testifies She Was Forced into Oral Sex." *Jet* magazine. August 28, 1975: 17–18. Print. Web accessed June 9, 2016.

Davis, Angela. "Joan Little: The Dialectics of Rape." *Ms.* magazine. June 1975. Print. www.msmagazine.com/spring2002/davis.asp.

Thomson, MaryJane. *Sarah Vaughan Is Not My Mother: A Memoir of Madness.* Wellington, New Zealand: Awa Press, 2013.

Abé, K. *Jazz Giants: A Visual Retrospective.* New York: Billboard Publications, 1988.

Shell-Weiss, Melanie, and Tammy Evans. "The Silencing of Ruby McCollum: Race, Class, and Gender in the South." *The Florida Historical Quarterly* 85, no. 4 (2007): 479–81.

Gottlieb, Robert, ed. *Reading Jazz: A Gathering of Autobiography, Reportage, and Criticism from 1919 to Now.* New York: Pantheon Books, 1996.

Royster, Francesca T. *Sounding Like a No-No: Queer Sounds and Eccentric Acts in the Post-Soul Era.* Ann Arbor: University of Michigan Press, 2013.

Kitt, Eartha. *Thursday's Child.* [1st ed.] New York: Duell, Sloan and Pearce, 1956.

Mezzack, Janet. "'Without Manners You Are Nothing': Lady Bird Johnson, Eartha Kitt, and the Women Doers' Luncheon of January 18, 1968." *Presidential Studies Quarterly* 20, no. 4 (1990): 745–60.

Billingsley, Andrew. *Mighty Like a River: The Black Church and Social Reform.* New York: Oxford University Press, 1999.

Gross, Kali N. *Colored Amazons: Crime, Violence, and Black Women in the City of Brotherly Love, 1880–1910.* Durham, N.C.: Duke University Press, 2006.

PHOTO CREDITS

p. 64: Wikimedia Commons

p. 80: By Carl Van Vechten, 1880–1964, photographer [copyrighted free use], via Wikimedia Commons

p. 84: Photo by FPG/Archive Photos/Getty Images

p. 88: By Hugo van Gelderen/Anefo (Nationaal Archief) [CC BY-SA 3.0 nl (https://creativecommons.org/licenses/by-sa/3.0/nl/deed.en)], via Wikimedia Commons

p. 92: New York Public Library Archives, the New York Public Library. "Sonia Sanchez," the New York Public Library Digital Collections, 1972. http://digitalcollections.nypl.org/items/6c8df720-49fc-5281-e040-e00a18062f9d

p. 96: Fibonacci Blue/Flickr

p. 102: Library of Congress

p. 106: Schlesinger Library, Radcliffe Institute, Harvard University

p. 110: *Pittsburgh Courier* Archives

p. 114: By Bruce from Sydney, Australia (Grace Jones) [CC BY 2.0 https://creativecommons.org/licenses/by/2.0], via Wikimedia Commons

p. 118: By Warren K. Leffler, *U.S. News & World Report*; restored by Adam Cuerden [public domain], via Wikimedia Commons

p. 124: Photo by © Bettmann/CORBIS/Bettmann Archive. Original caption.

p. 138: Rachael Garner

A Note on the Author

DaMaris B. Hill is assistant professor of creative writing and African American and Africana studies at the University of Kentucky. Her previous works are *The Fluid Boundaries of Suffrage and Jim Crow: Staking Claims in the American Heartland* and a collection of poetry, *Vi-zə-bəl**Teks-chərs*\. She has two PhDs, one in English and one in women and gender studies. A former service member of the United States Air Force, she lives in Lexington, Kentucky.